Said Alhosni is a distinguished expert in Human Resources Management, celebrated for his exceptional contributions across four diverse sectors. With a career marked by high achievements, Said brings a wealth of experience and insight to his writing, making him a sought-after voice in his field.

In *Twenty Lessons,* Said's second book, he shares ten profound lessons drawn from his rich personal, professional, and social experiences. This book not only serves as a guide to personal and professional growth but also as a heartfelt tribute to his late parents and His Majesty Qaboos bin Said, whose legacies he aims to honor and immortalize.

Said's journey into authorship began with an ambitious attempt at writing an Arabic book, a project that remains a testament to his dedication to sharing knowledge. He has also contributed thought-provoking articles to the national initiative أقلام الشباب, showcasing his commitment to youth empowerment and intellectual discourse.

Twenty Lessons is more than just a book; it is a bridge between Said's personal narrative and the universal lessons that resonate with us all. Through his stories, readers will find inspiration, practical advice, and a deep sense of connection.

Follow Said on Instagram @_said_alhosni or reach out via email at said-alhosni@outlook.sa for more insights and updates on his work.

To my mom and dad, I cannot put into words how grateful I
am for what both of you have done for me.

Big thanks to my wife and daughters.

Big thanks to my brothers and sisters.

Big thanks to my few close friends.

Said Nasser Alhosni

TWENTY LESSONS IN APRIL

AUSTIN MACAULEY PUBLISHERS®

LONDON ∗ CAMBRIDGE ∗ NEW YORK ∗ SHARJAH

ISBN – 9789948748649 – (Paperback)
ISBN – 9789948748656 – (E-Book)

Application Number: MC-10-01-3834228
Age Classification: E

The age group that matches the content of the books has been classified according to the age classification system issued by the UAE Media Council.

Printer Name: iPrint Global Ltd
Printer Address: Witchford, England

First Published 2024
AUSTIN MACAULEY PUBLISHERS FZE
Sharjah Publishing City
P.O Box [519201]
Sharjah, UAE
www.austinmacauley.ae
+971 655 95 202

Self-Reflection

When I decided to write this book, I put together a plan because I knew from first-hand experience that it is not easy to do it. I knew it would be impossible to go on without encountering any challenges and setbacks.

I laid down the plan because I once attempted to write a small book almost eight years ago. I had already started writing it but, unfortunately, I could not finish it for many reasons. One of the reasons is that there was no plan, and the other reason is that it had no purpose.

What I did differently this time compared with that previous small book which I intended to write before were two things:

1. I put together a plan and made SMART goals.
2. I chose someone with excellent skills in writing to check my work, and who could coach and mentor me at the same time.

If you ask me how I was finally able to finish this project, my answer would be because of the above-mentioned two points. Then, the secondary reasons would be that this book is my passion, and because it is my lifelong dream. I can say that this book helped me get to know myself deeply, especially when I was trying to dig up more about my history.

Some topics in this book are very personal to me; they really moulded my character and changed my life. Moreover, writing this book also allowed me to see how I perceive tasks. I discovered that my mood has an impact on my desire to write, as I am bit moody and it is not always easy for me to focus on long-term projects.

What I wrote in this small book really meant a lot to me because each topic changed and added something valuable within me.

Trust me when I say some of them were not easy to write and think about. I am sure there are still more stories I can write about between these lines but some incidents I still do not dare to share with people. This is why I expected that some of you, my readers, will have a lot of questions about some topics and points in my book. I believe that curiosity and passion are the keys to know yourself. This is why I advise you to not hesitate to dig deeper about your past incidents and stories in your life, because your personality today is a great by-product of those incidents and stories.

Writing is one of the great ways to uncover and unearth deep emotions you have kept hidden all these years within yourself. In fact, before I started to write this book, I thought it was easy to remember everything, but honestly, it was not. I observed that it was difficult to write those episodes, especially the ones that were emotionally painful and even drastically life-changing.

In addition, having the right focus and concentration is not easy to achieve, especially during the COVID-19 pandemic and recent natural disasters like the Shaheen Cyclone which affected Oman. These sudden and natural phenomena surely created a strong impact on the entire humanity, either negatively or positively.

How I wish I had more time with myself by writing other lessons and stories, either dismal or great memories.

This book in your hand might lead you to see someone faced with the same incidents and challenges as I did. It might force you to remember something in your history that can help you answer your purpose. I started with this question to myself… why am I here?

Happy reading and my best wishes to you.

Chapter 1
There Is Revolution for
Each New Journey

In every life journey, we will encounter episodes, events, and circumstances that will knock us out and shock us. Primarily because these events were unexpected, unforeseen, and unplanned. But like it or not, we have to accept that it has always been part of our fate. This is the reason why I call it a REVOLUTION.

It is a revolution because it is indeed life-changing. The impact that it has created is something so hard for us to believe or even digest. But let us bear in mind that however unfortunate it may look from the outside, we should remember that there are fortunate results that can come out of these unfortunate events and it all depends on us.

These events can be a death of a loved one, a horrible accident, end of a relationship, loss of job, or bankruptcy. The physical and emotional turmoil it causes you can make you feel that you are on a pit of a dark hole, so tiny that you cannot breathe. You feel you are drowning.

I remember the story of my mother. It happened when I was 18 years old. I did not expect I will be able to overcome this tragic event. It never occurred to me at all because it was something I was not expecting to happen.

I can still vividly remember very well that night. My mother was with me until 2 o'clock in the morning. She was begging me to accept something that was related to my future. When I finally relented and accepted, she told my sister, "I can now sleep well. At least I convinced him."

Days prior to this incident, she took me with her to teach me how to buy fish and food for my brothers and sisters. This is why I patterned all her ways and words on how I conduct myself.

I will go back to that night when she was convincing me. I remember seeing her in front of me. She was laughing and covering her face with her blanket. She was acting like a giddy child. I was wondering what happened to her and why she is behaving like that because it was my first time to see her act that way. After our heart-to-heart conversation, I went back to my bed to sleep.

Suddenly in the morning, I was awakened from sleep because I heard some strange voice. I went to check on my mother. There I saw her lying down on the floor.

I could not believe what I saw before my eyes. So I ran like crazy and I rushed screaming towards my brother's room. I knocked his door forcefully until he opened the door. I was shouting and panicking, and I said to my brother, "Our mom… there, please do something. Come see her!" Then he ran to see what happened to her and he was shocked too and he got her in his arms… he was trying to talk to her, but there was no answer.

After that, he took her to the hospital. From that day on, she neither talked nor opened her eyes. What difficult days those were without her! Every call was making me feel nervous.

Then one morning, I received the call from my brother, he told me, "Said, our mother passed away."

I couldn't control myself during those moments. She was my life. I can still remember hearing my sisters crying and I couldn't do something about it.

It was one year. One year that I cried, grieved and I felt so alone. I couldn't accept that she was gone just like that. After one year, I told myself I had to make a decision, either to spoil my life forever or to turn it around.

I decided to think properly. I felt a revolution occurring inside me that gave birth to my new life journey.

This one life-changing story from hundreds of stories which gave me a strong message and lesson. I observed that most of the accidents happened to us for a reason.

Yes, in the beginning, we will not accept what happened but after some time we will observe that there is a reason that will change us and eventually we will become better version of ourselves.

I like to refer to the words of one author, Neil Donald, who said, "When everything changes, change everything." These accidents gave me indication that I needed to change radically.

Now I am wondering what my life would have been like had that unfortunate calamity not struck me. This is why I thanked Allah for what had happened.

I met a lot of people who gave up because of similar stories and they decided to change for the worse. They took what happened to them negatively which was not right at all. They need to think wisely when tragedy strikes.

Life is about a continuous journey of decision-making. Whatever comes our way, it is our decision whether we take it negatively or handle it wisely. In the end, it is you who will go up or down.

I will tell you my story and I will not deny the fact that when I recall this incident in my life, I feel some tinge of regret.

One day, I decided to leave the company where I was working. I aimed to join another company which offered me a higher position and I considered it a big leap in my career. In the first two weeks in my new job, I felt there was something odd with some people working there. Then, as days and weeks passed, I discovered my initial feelings were right. I felt under pressure because of the strange attitude of my coworkers. Because of that, I decided to leave as I could not tolerate what they were doing to me. I resigned from that job and I should say I gave them the golden plate free of any resistance from me.

Today, as I understand the rules of the game in the workplace, we need to be a strong fighter, both psychologically and emotionally. It was easier to just give up and quit.

Sometimes, we give up without standing up against what we feel is not right. We give up without any form of resistance that will give rise to such feelings as regret in the future.

Actually, it is great when we face any challenge in our life, whether small or big. We need to think and come up with more than one option and to be honest with ourselves with these options which will steer us to right or wrong track. In this way, it will help us to think and to change our minds to follow the right steps. I know by now that I will not always win but at least I put up a good fight. At least, we must think that the trials that will come our way will give us lessons and worthy experience.

Looking back, I should have told myself back then that I should not give up just like that. Therefore, I tell you now, put in your mind as a rule that there is no challenge that should be faced by giving up. We need to keep digging deep down our inner strength to overcome the adversaries. I believe that this is the way to reach the level of satisfaction and without regret.

Lesson:

Bear in mind that in every revolution arises a new life journey. So learn from the lessons of the trials and tribulations that come your way, and be wise to make the right decision so you will live your life with satisfaction.

Chapter 2
My Weapon Is Passion

Life is anything but perfect. There will be derails, bumps and detours along the way. That is if you have not clearly defined what you really want to pursue or what you are passionate about, you will find yourself easily lost and desolate. So I say in all these challenges in your life, you should have a powerful weapon to wield off the thorns in your path and to weather out the storms. A weapon that is so strong that you can hold on to clear away your path. For me, **my weapon is passion.**

What is passion? Passion is a strong and powerful feeling that gives rise to emotions such as love, desire and devotion. Passion is based on our own experience.

Realistically speaking, it can go up and or it can go down. It can shut down or diminish but all you need to do is re-focus once again. We need to link it to the decision that we have to make.

My message is: do not wait for passion to come to you. You need to attract passion. You have to have the desire. You need to work hard to gain passion by having a goal and target in life.

To harness that passion in you, you should also put in consideration that you have to have the positive attitude, practice growth mindset, and surround yourself with passionate people.

If there are factors that fuel passion, on the other hand, I can say, there are also factors that can kill passion. These can be people, surroundings around you, choices that you make that can kill passion such as negativity, laziness, having no goals and no dreams… no purpose.

When I was taking up my Masters in Business Administration (MBA), most of us in that class were employed. Balancing the demand of work and studies was not easy to achieve.

Then came one day, one of my classmates was close to quitting because he could not manage to work and study at the same time. He told me that he cannot continue and he is going to withdraw his documents from the college.

When he told me that, I decided to do something about it. I cheered him up. I told him to listen to me and I told him to imagine that he is on the stage in graduation ceremony after two years. Then, I continued telling him, "Picture out one best and close person to you and that person was there seeing you. See that person, smiling proudly at you." I told him, "Don't you think that this scenario deserves you to fight hard for and to continue? So that you are able to live this scenario until it becomes reality one day?"

After that conversation, he looked at me then he said, "You are right and you are great, it is indeed a wonderful feeling!"

Hence that person, my classmate, decided to strive hard to complete his MBA. We studied together most of the time.

Then came our graduation day, I was very happy to see him with his mother there in our graduation ceremony. The passion needs us to visualize a real picture to keep reminding us and lead us to the right direction where we are heading.

During one of my training sessions, I told my trainees that passion needs fuel otherwise it will be lost one day. I know you are asking yourself, "How?"

Do not misunderstand me; what I mean without action there is no passion. This is why when there is no action, I can say the passion is fake.

Let us be honest with ourselves, there is no dream without hard work and this why we need passion to be able to continue. Passion is the fuel when you feel especially, when you look at your picture that you have plan of accomplishing. After fulfilling that goal, you can hear yourself exclaiming, "What a feeling!"

Many people keep asking me how I can work like that and never stop. My answer is and remains consistent. "It is passion and you do not know what I see and feel when I keep chasing and working on my goal… indeed, what a feeling!"

On the contrary, you will observe there are some people in your school or workplace who lost their passion because they had expectations from their professors or their managers and these expectations were not met. Then as a result, they become frustrated, demotivated and lost. Primarily because they allow their passion to be attached to another person (such as their boss, their parents or someone they look up to) and not on their own selves. If that person is gone, they will be disheartened and this will diminish their passion.

There are circumstances when I asked some people about "What is your goal or purpose?" There is one former colleague of mine whom I met again after five years and I asked him the same question. I was surprised. He gave me the same answer with the same goal without any progress. I must say I was shocked.

I do understand that without the passion this is the result as always, people keep on postponing their actions. This is what happens when you allow yourself to depend on other people for your passion in life. Because as good as people may seem, like your manager or leader or friend, they will not be permanent in your life. It is not in their hands to lead you or be there for you the whole time. They will move, they will go to another workplace because by nature people come and go. The sooner you realize and accept that, the better for you.

I have my **3 P's** that I live by **Passion**, **Professional,** and **Polite**. These are my principles in life. Passion for me matters a lot because it is what makes an ordinary person become extraordinary. It is the one that drives the person to think out of the box, to become creative and to challenge the norm.

Sometimes it's craziness, I should say. But like Steve Jobs – who created the Apple iPhone and MacBook – once said that you should be crazy enough to believe that you can change the world.

Passion is what sets apart the people who can add value to their company or business from those who just go with the flow of life.

Lesson:

Passion should emanate from you. It should be self-motivated.

Chapter 3
Difficult Conversation:
It Is a Make or Break

If you take a look at it and ask ourselves, how many times have we had difficult conversation with our managers, co-workers, family, and friends? We know for a fact that all of these conversations were really difficult to begin with but however difficult it may seem, the goal should not be to end it badly.

A couple of years ago, I conducted a workshop with my colleagues on how to handle difficult conversation with people around us. This is one reason why I chose this topic.

I realized that many people around us are not aware about the consequences that can result if we do not know how to manage these crucial moments in our personal and professional life.

In my own point of view, many relationships break or lead to distorted relationships because of the lack of knowledge in handling difficult conversations.

Therefore, after long search and living with many such incidents, I believe that difficult confrontation will happen at one point in our lives either now or later. It may be at home, in workplace, or along the way, hence we have to have a good knowledge of it, prepare for it and practice handling it.

On the other hand, I realized too that no matter how many times you have handled difficult conversations in the past, it will not always be easy to manage it. Based on my experience, the success or failure of the confrontation will depend on you.

Hence, I am here to share with you these lessons and guidelines for you to come out successful after the difficult conversation. The need to have difficult conversation arises in various cases such as we feel disappointment when expectations were not met, such as ambiguity, low performance, promises were broken, or when there is an exchange of insulting words or actions, and the lists goes on.

That means, in most cases, anger or disappointment in heightened state is our emotional condition at that crucial time. This is the main reason why it is important to know how to strategize for you to reach your valued goal.

Here are the crucial steps in handling difficult conversations. Firstly, one thing we should do is to clarify our objective or goal before we start the conversation. Ask yourself, "What is my purpose for this talk? Is it about improving performance or relationship? Or is it to steer someone important to you back on the right track?"

You should know the state, the purpose, and be clear with that. This matter should be clear in order for you to be able to do the right thing and say the right words regardless of their reaction.

Secondly, clarify with the person if it is the right time to have such conversation. Check if the other person is in bad mood or if there are other people present, which is not good to open the conversation; wherein usually such scenarios happen.

Thirdly, after starting the conversation, do not expect the other person will be convinced immediately and this is why it is important that you are ready for their reaction.

In addition, it is also beneficial to lead the conversation by asking smart questions which will make it easier for you to convince the other person. You can ask question like, "What do you think will happen if you continue" or "Don't you see that it will cause some damage to you?"

Here is a story that happened to me one day when we were gathering for a big family feast. One of my relatives, intruded in the middle of my conversations with my other family members. He did it in an offensive manner and his voice was loud. He was recollecting about one incident that happened a long time ago and there was already a miscommunication about certain details from the start.

In short, there was a misunderstanding. The manner and tone of his delivery made me feel embarrassed in front of my whole family. That is the reason why my reaction was to fire back at him with an even louder voice. Then I walked out. I know my reaction was very aggressive.

Now if I'd ask myself, "Was his actions right? Was my reaction appropriate?" All of these questions were in my mind after that incident and I am sure you faced similar stories like mine. If you handled it well, I would like to salute you. It was not about whose mistake was it, but in the end, the confrontation wasn't handled well and there was exaggerated reaction from me.

On the other hand, in my career path for the last 13 years, I have worked with one manager who'd always belittle me and he was such a bully who enjoyed ridiculing and teasing me all the time. There were instances when he would embarrass me in front of my team. I felt that this has to stop.

So one day, I found the courage to talk to him. I knew I will engage him in a difficult conversation knowing his attitude and temper.

I reminded myself to stick to my principles, the two out of three Ps principles which I live by, which are Professional and Polite. I told him that I did not like his words and actions towards me and I will not accept it the next time. He asked me what I did not like. So I enumerated it to him…1, 2, 3.

After that difficult conversation, he apologized and said he was sorry. I am proud to say it was successful because I managed the difficult conversation with him wisely.

I always confronted him when he treated me in a bad way. After I confronted him, he will change for a few days but then he will repeat his ways all over again.

When I got another opportunity to move to another company, before I resigned, I expressed my feelings with him once again for the last time just to make him aware about his ways and the consequences of his actions.

What I want to say here is that difficult conversation is a make or break. It is either you come out of it feeling better and coming up with a win-win solution or it can destroy a relationship.

What I learned from these stories, firstly, is that it is very important to know the right time to have a difficult conversation. Because sometimes people will consider that discussion to be an insult or an attack on them.

This is why you need to ask permission first from the concerned party if it is the right time to discuss. What I mean here is when I want to discuss about something such as fixing a relationship, improving work performance or the like, you need to ask the other person if it this time is a good time to talk about the matter of concern.

Secondly, you need to stick to the facts of the matter at hand. You should not use past stories or other people which or who are not relevant and can just make matters worse.

Thirdly, I learned from my second story about my manager that it is not about who win in the confrontation but it is about gaining the proper skills in order to fix the professional relationship.

I know many people keep it in their hearts when someone treats them in bad way and do not confront the person. However, this is not right. We need to be bold enough and be brave to engage in the difficult conversation.

I believe being able to handle a difficult conversation is a great skill to have. This is why people who had triumph over trials and experience difficult conversations, have the strongest capability to fix their personal and professional relationship and also their work performance.

Lesson:

Difficult conversation is not for the sake of discussion. During difficult conversation, once we engage on it with a clear sense of purpose, we will gain a lot from it. It is important that we know how to approach and handle it.

Chapter 4
Between the Starting and Finishing Line of a Goal

One day, someone said to me this, "I have a goal but I do not know how to achieve it. What do you think is the issue?"My response is, "What is the purpose of this goal?"

He: Just like that.

Me: The issue here is, if you do not put high value in the purpose of your goal, you will not be able to work on it consistently.

More likely, the same stories are repeated in our lives on a daily basis. The basic issue is because there is no real motivation to achieve it. It is not clear in our mind, if the goal is aligned with our purpose; then what do you think will it happen?

Let me recollect one point in the past when I was in school, particularly when I was in my ninth year, when we were made to choose which subjects we had to take for years 11 and 12, arts, math, or science.

At that time, many students chose their specialization based on the choices of their friends so that they can still be together. I believe young as we are at this is a crucial stage, we are tested on how we will progress with our life especially in our future.

We have to make independent decisions as early at that. But unfortunately, others go with the flow and follow the tide like a dead fish. Their goal was more to have time with friends than defining what they want to achieve in the future.

I am fortunate that my friend and I had different rules in our friendship. Each one of us chose his specialization freely based on our own interests and the field we thought we will excel in.

At that point, I chose arts because maths was very hard for me. On the other hand, he opted for maths class. The question to begin with was, how come some people put their selves in such situation with no goal for their own self and just follow the shadow of others.

Here is the secret. This is why it is very important that we need to know ourselves… our strengths and weaknesses because many people put goals because they compare themselves with others. Also, some fail because they chose goals which are not achievable at all.

I am happy today because I set my goal to accomplish this book. Before I started, I put the purpose and the number of days I needed to finish. Moreover, I divided this goal by 30 weeks and each week I to finished a specific topic.

This is why every Saturday I celebrate when I achieve 100%. Imagine a big goal which I cut and sub-divide into small goals to be able to achieve the big one.

Do you think by this way you will quit? I do not think so. In fact, all the more you will be motivated to work more and celebrate your success on a weekly basis.

In addition, one valuable 'ingredient' which I added this time in this book project is to ask someone for support as I knew how significant it is. I asked one of the best writers I have ever met in my life and we worked on this together. She is Ms. Monera Lukman. She is the one who I trust blindly and I am sure with her writing skills she will make this book amazing with the help of her wisdom.

Therefore, my advice to you, one of the instrumental keys to achieve your goals is that you will need someone around you who has the right skills to assist you in successfully materializing your goal.

I will open up to you my story that I have kept secret for a long time. I set this goal to write my book four years ago. During the last four years, I tried to achieve this but by initiating different ways and it seemed, I was going nowhere and I did not progress. I could not do it.

Now I know the reason based on what I have shared with you about setting goals. Now I know the secret formula of success, this is why I strongly believe that I will succeed in finishing this book.

Between the starting line and finishing line of achieving your goal is learning. Also, having someone to guide and motivate you will help you move towards your finish line.

As you start to embark on your goal, you will be passing through several tests. When you are hurdling these tests, it is trial and error, you will make mistakes. Failure is part of the steps. Yes, failures can be frustrating, cumbersome and disappointing. But remember this: **there are more lessons in losses than wins.**

It is how you manage these failures and it is from these mistakes that you will learn. So do not allow failures to stop you. Learn from it and move on.

Lesson:

Because I failed, I learned.

Highly Valued Purpose + Focus + Time-Bound = Goal Achieved

Chapter 5
Worrying: All of a Sudden,
I Found Myself Worried

When I was in elementary school, I heard the word 'worry' mentioned by people around me. Back then, I did not know exactly what it means. Along the way when I was growing up, I found myself sometimes feeling tense and not relax especially when waiting for something like, for instance my score in an exam or my grades in secondary school.

I noticed that the state of being worried was with me especially every time I embarked on a new stage in my life. I remember, I was worried before I started college. I was worried when I was looking for job, when I had a bad manager, when one of my close relatives was sick, when I did not have money, when I compared myself with others and I was worried before I got up on the stage to deliver my speech.

The reason why I am writing this topic is that it is very crucial to understand when we have to accept the feeling of being worried. I say this because for me, there are two types of worry.

One type of worry is that it will push you up while the other type is the kind of worry that will drag you down.

I would like to share to you one story that I think most of you can relate. One day, one of my friends invited me to his place, and when I reached there he told me that the reason he brought me with him is because his friend had a big problem. So I asked his friend, "What is your problem?"

He replied to me, "Just that I am not happy at all and I always worry about my life."

After our long conversation, I discovered there is nothing wrong with this guy. Nothing happened to him but just his way of thinking which kept him always worried for nothing.

Let me ask you: Do you think this guy will be able to achieve what he wants? What do you think, how will he live his life with this way of thinking?

On the other hand, I will share to you the opposite story of worry. As I told you, I worry a lot before I go up the stage to conduct a training or do public speaking. Four years ago, I told my general manager, Mr. Charles Saliba, that one of my life goals is to become a motivational speaker. He was not only my GM, but I look at him as my mentor and coach because he was the one who supported and pushed me to go for it.

I remember that he put me many times in awkward situations in the past such as letting me conduct a training session, when at the beginning I thought to myself I cannot make it happen.

The one moral lesson I learned from this experience is that worry has a healthy side with this kind of situation because without worry you will not care. Without worry, you will not dare to move and improve yourself. Without the good side of worry, you will accept mediocrity and it will lead you nowhere.

Moreover, I realize that worry also keeps on teaching me that when I feel it, it means there is something that needs to be changed or improved. Sometimes, it is an advance warning or sign to prioritize an important task.

For instance, I had this feeling. When worry got to me, I took it as a warning that I need to review my schedule. True enough, my schedule really needs to be cleared out from tasks that are not important and not urgent because I have a crucial task to accomplish that day.

Therefore, do not allow the worry to consume you but use it to keep you guarded, on your toes and use it to warn you to follow what you should prioritize more.

In order to do away with worry, you need to think ahead. Nothing beats than being prepared. Preparation is key to success. Also, knowledge is power that will make you combat worry.

The worry will occur but you need to know how to dust it off from your shoulders then motivate yourself to know where you are going and move forward.

Combat the worry by daring to go beyond your self-doubt and fears. Seek knowledge, for knowledge is power. Preparation is key to make you ready to face the challenges ahead. Use worry as an advance warning, a sign or whatever you call it, to prepare you well for things that is within your control. But for things or events beyond your control, let them be.

Lesson:

Look at worry as a positive sign. Handle the tasks where you feel worried and face it head on. Prioritize the situation that is urgent and important because most likely this is the one causing you to feel worried. Seek knowledge and seek help if you must.

Chapter 6
It Is Just Matter of Time

It is a long journey with time. All stories that I mentioned in this book took some time. It is either they happened a long time ago or it took a length of time for me to be ready to talk about it and to share it openly. These stories like about my career path where I was and who I become today, like when I lost my mother, father, or friends. Even, when I made wrong decisions and its consequences chased me for long time.

I meant stories that I needed time until I achieved the happiness I longed for. Or stories which I lived that had me feeling so much pain and I needed long time to overcome it until I forgot the pain that caused me. This is why, for me, time has its own high value in life because we need to allow time to reveal the true essence of the incident or the phenomenon and the lessons brought along by it.

Negative life events require time for us to heal the wounds, and overcome the pain and finally let go and live triumphantly with so much joy and happiness.

All of us have 24 hours but there is a big difference between those who invest the time in the right way and those who wasted it. I cannot forget the time when I was dreaming to achieve one of my goals and how many times I was close to quitting.

Fortunately, there was an inner voice within me that was telling me, "Just be patient, it is just a matter of time." I followed that voice and I succeeded.

I have heard from work, in the park or at home and even within me that I cannot wait but I realize that if we cannot be patient with time, we will not be able achieve our dreams or forget our pain. I remember once I was working in one of the companies where I suffered a lot and I learnt a lot too, now I am surprised that I have that power to resist in that difficult time.

The good thing I had was hope that I am not in that situation for nothing but surely Allah kept something for me there. This is why I sacrificed and persevered without looking at all at the negative happening circumventing it.

I learnt that all wounds need time to recover and time to heal... always. These people who are successful is not because they have all the luck, but they are the ones who were strong and who kept themselves focused on how to make themselves more adaptable during these difficult situations.

The one thing that kept me wondering is that how my parents were very strong to handle their time with more than 12 children and I can see the fruits of their labor until now.

My mother shared to me many difficult stories that happened to her at the times which I was not aware of. Definitely it was not easy to pass all of those difficult situations.

One of the stories that were a real tragedy was when my father was put in jail because it came to a point that he was broke.

My mother had nothing but my oldest brother and sister. After a long time, she sought to meet our beloved His Majesty Sultan Qaboos. When my mother brought to his attention the situation, he paid all my father's loans to get him out of the jail.

If my mother was not patient then and did not believe to wait for the right time, do you think my great mother could succeed? I can guarantee that at that time the one thing she was holding on to was her firm belief on the compassion and benevolence of His Majesty Sultan Qaboos that he will help her.

Moreover, this is why she invested her time despite her tough and difficult situation to meet him. Because of the tremendous help she received from His Majesty, she devoted her entire life to him, always talking proudly about His Majesty. What a feeling of pride to have someone like Sultan Qaboos to have walked on this earth and became the highest leader of Oman. May Allah bring them to heaven.

Lesson:

The lesson here is that you face different kinds difficulties in this life either personal, professional, financial, health-related, but how you handle the situation and how you invest your time will always make the difference. Whatever situation you are in, I tell you, do not lose hope and just keep on going. Be patient because it will happen and it will be revealed, it is just a matter of time.

Chapter 7
My Failures Made Me

It is needless to say that most of us have fear of failing because of how we see failure. To fail is to be a loser. To fail is a mistake. To fail is something negative. To fail is wrong.

That is the reason why if you read the history of most of the people, you will see that they did not take big leaps and made risky decisions because of the number one fear… the fear of failure.

They are ZERO people taking risky steps in their life. They choose to stay in their comfort zone. But you can always hear them complaining about their work, their salary, and their miseries.

In order to feel good, they put the blame on someone else… maybe on the management, on their bosses, their colleagues; on the kind of family they were born into or maybe their fate. They complain why they are still where they are until now. But what they do not see is that they are afraid to take action, to ask for more responsibilities or to talk to their boss and negotiate for a raise.

Because the truth is, it is easier to blame than to take action. They have a lot of fears in their mind. In fact, failure in the form of rejection or losing; it is a major concern that they are trying to avoid.

It is true; it is not easy to accept our own failures but we must accept it like in our marriage vows, we have to be willing to go through it for better or for worse, through thick and thin… with our very own self.

As it is, this is the life. But the truth of the matter is, if only we know how to look at failure positively, see it as an opportunity than a loss and to handle it successfully, we can turn it around and it will be a big reason to propel us towards our own success.

I am proud here to tell you about my father's story. My mother told me this story of before I was born. She said, "Your dad was a rich man but suddenly because of some circumstances he became broke to the point that he landed himself in jail." Why I am telling you this story is because in my whole life, I never felt that my dad had undergone such failure.

I saw him as a man who is very hard working until the end of his life. In my mind, I am sure he had the option when he got out of the jail to stay negative without doing anything. But he chose to keep doing great things after his coming out of jail.

He was able to bounce back and acquire a big house and other notable material possessions. I am wondering now what was in his mind when he got in the jail and after he got out of it.

I can guarantee that definitely he had his own philosophy in handling failures. Because I saw in him, not a man who is a failure but a man who was tough enough to overcome his failures and rise up again.

Based on my experience, failure is not always failing. Most of the time, failure is a state of feeling. We are the one labeling ourselves with it. I remembered when I lost my own small business due to my health; it took me one year until I recovered. I was blaming myself as I saw myself as a failure.

After long time, I discovered that actually I was not a failure. Actually, those difficult circumstances that I lost my business and I got sick, led me to see a dozen of lessons.

Without these mistakes, the wrong decisions I made, I would not be who I am today. Thus, we need to have a philosophy in our life to accept that mistakes are part of how we live our life. Failure is not the end of our life, it is a re-direction or re-awakening that we are being led to a different path that will be best for us.

We just have to know how to see it and avoid looking at it as a shock especially when we cannot get what we want.

On the other hand, do not forget that there are people who are waiting for you to fail and stop. They will use these words 'you will fail' to make you feel down. Some of them may not mean it but to be honest, human as we are, it will affect our feelings.

Therefore, be careful when you are thinking, talking and taking actions. 'You will fail' are toxic words and these words can affect your thinking, your determination, and your future, if you allow them.

Hence, in order for you to succeed, you must need to have proper psychological relationship with your own self… with your mind and with your heart.

The lesson is that failing should be something we need to accept that can happen. But we should not allow failure to stop us or end the strength that is left of us. We should not allow failure to define the end of who we are. We should see failure as a lesson that we need to learn from and not to repeat.

Look at failure as a stumbling block that we need to re-energize and re-charge our spirits. Enhance your knowledge, take up new skills, and regain back your self-confidence. Otherwise, if you allow failure to stop you, to dampen your spirits, you are definitely headed towards the wrong path.

Lift yourself up and pick up the pieces. Make failure as your key to open new doors and opportunities to bounce back and write your own success story.

Lesson:

I learned from my mistakes, my wrong decisions, my 'not so well-thought-out' plans and choices. Looking back, without these failures, I will not be stronger, wiser, not even bold enough to take gigantic jumps and take risks.

I will not be who I am today, without my failures. I accept that my failures are my lessons in my life. Hence it is with great pride that I say, 'My failures made me.'

Chapter 8
The Year of Shock and Loss

I like to start by telling you that I already experienced feeling one of the worse possible feelings any human being can feel and go through. This happened at one point in my life.

One day when I was inside my French class; suddenly, a horrible feeling took hold of me, which made me drive as fast as I could to reach the hospital.

When I got there, I immediately ran to the doctor who was shocked when she saw me in front of her. She asked me, "What happened to you? Where were you? Someone chased you?"

I replied to the doctor, "No, no… just I feel am dying."

From that moment on, everything changed. All of a sudden, I changed. I became not that optimistic person. I suffered for one year as I was looking for my treatment and I knocked on all the doors.

One year, I felt alone in the middle of the crowd and fears were coming from everywhere. I felt like I was left alone in the corner. It was one year, I looked at the life from different corners.

During that year, I felt I was looking at life from another set of eyes and ears. I felt that I was trapped inside a locked bottle of water where I was struggling desperately to gasp for air and move up. The feeling inside was that I could not see any hope and no chance of surviving. I could not focus on anything and my mind was nowhere… it was up and down.

During my course of treatment, for the first three months, the storm was controlling me. For the second three months, people who are around were the ones who were controlling me. For the third three months, my thoughts were fighting to help me to get rid of something but I could not find anything to focus on them.

For the last three months, I started understanding my inner voice which tried to get my attention but because of nothing it could not. I can say I lost in those difficult months as I pity myself because of those terrible thoughts which made me feel lost and feeling nowhere.

What a tremendous challenge it was! To get rid of those fake feelings. I was asking myself, where am I? I went into deep thinking until I realized that the solution is within me and not with someone else. To be honest, I cannot precisely find the words to put all the details to be able to write openly about it.

The bottom-line is: my goal here is that I like to share my story so I can give my advice which may help people who experienced shock in their life and thought they cannot continue, and eventually succumbed into depression.

In such situation, do not give in and you should believe that there are people who are ready to stand with you and support you until you survive and recover. The most important advice also which I like to share is that do not leave what you love doing, whatever it may be small or big endeavors such as sports, reading, painting, or anything that still makes you happy doing.

Despite my situation during that time, I did not stop attending my French class where I could feel I was still alive. Hold on to the things important to you that will keep you to feel alive despite your state of depression.

I would like to sincerely thank all the people who supported me in that crucial phase in my life to be able to overcome my psychological crises. It was one of the most difficult battles that was extremely hard to be in. I am proud of myself because I won in my war with depression as I hear a lot of people lost their war.

On this note, I can truly say giving up is never an option. You have to choose to be strong to fight your own battle. Continue fighting until you win in the end.

Best regards, the fighter.

Chapter 9
ME Time'

One day, we will reach to the point in our lives where we feel we need to sit down with ourselves. Most of the time, we make time for other people, we give them our attention, our care and most of all… our time.

But let me ask you, how often did you give time for yourself? When was the last time did you actually give attention and talk to yourself? Do you ever engage in self-reflection? Have you thought that today it will be my time for myself… my 'ME time.'

Unfortunately, some people resort to doing crazy things to escape and to find an exit to the problems they are in. They drink, they gamble, they do drugs just to look for that escape, that euphoria, that high, thinking that this kind of vices will let them forget their problems.

Yes temporarily, it will. But the problem is still looming there the next morning. Or, in fact, it might be even worse.

They do not give themselves space even once a month or maybe even once a year to reflect on themselves.

My advice is give space for yourself to give time to self-reflect, evaluate and get to know your direction or goals in life.

You can look around you and you will see these people have many issues like family issues, financial issues, work issues, self-issues and spiritual issues. But ask them, "Did you stop and think a bit of what can help you resolve these issues? Did you ask yourself what do you really want in life for you to be happy?"

I agree that most of us have some degree of craziness in certain times of our life. I must confess that I, myself, have my own share of craziness. However, I am sure no one wants his life like that but sometimes because they continued having the same habits for long time that they reach to the intangible prison where they cannot get rid of them.

I can say to these people that there are still a million chances to start again from the beginning. It is never too late to change your direction when it comes to steering yourself to the right track.

I will share with you my short story when I decided to have my own program which I called it… 'Me in 90 days.' It was in 2019, I quit to do many habits that I used to do which I believe were not healthy. These are one of toughest 90 days I have had to go through. I pushed myself to read books about self-change that motivated and helped me a lot. I put in my mind that I will not be able to stop all habits but at least achieving 65% of my goal will make feeling satisfied.

I am proud of my '90 days project' because I noticed that the quality of my life and my kind of self is a better version than it was before.

In 2020, I built my own plan for the next ten years to achieve my target which before I looked at it as not possible to achieve. Therefore, I believe that we need time with ourselves, to self-reflect and to ask ourselves where are we going in the next 10 years. It will improve our quality of life by which give result to good outcomes. It's not 100% guaranteed but there are certain degrees of certainty that it will.

Behaviors, attitudes, habits, and deeds always need time to sit down and assess with ourselves to improve them and make them better. Also the lesson here is do not believe when you hear someone say, "I do not have time for that."

I believe it is a matter of priority. Don't you think that you deserve such priority too? I will end here by saying that 'ME time' is the best investment you can ever give to yourself. Do it for yourself and not for anyone else. In the end, your future self will thank you for that.

Chapter 10
Road to Success Stick with the One Who Complements You Rather Than Who Just Compliments You

If we conduct a survey now and ask people, what type of manager they think they like to work with? A manager who is kind or the one who is strong? A kind manager will offer you compliment and praises. But a strong manager will tell straight to your face what you needed to hear which maybe you do not like to hear.

Someone who sees a bigger vision of you and would like to help you by giving you an honest feedback of how you need to improve and work on yourself. Some of us will feel bad or hurt of the reality they see but we must see the rhyme and reason behind what they are doing.

Some of us are struggling with our relationship and this can be a reason. We think that this kind of manager is the right leader for us. The one who offers you compliments but is reluctant to tell you what are your flaws and weaknesses.

They tell you what YOU WANT to hear but maybe not what YOU NEEDED to hear. A **strong manager is the one who will be straightforward to you**. Who is willing to tell you upfront your missing points or your weaknesses hoping that you will use this knowledge to help you see yourself and guide you along the way.

I noticed that in the workplace, most of the employees prefer to have a kind manager which is good for them for a time being but not for their future. I learned that strong managers are more beneficial for your career development than having kind managers.

What I mean here is, strong managers are those who are always straight-shooter and give honest feedback to let you see clearly where you stand and how to go ahead with your goal. If you see the positive side of it, this feedback is valuable tool to make you stronger and move up to your career.

I cannot forget Mr. Charles Saliba, who was my general manager in one company I worked for. He was the one who laid down the foundation of my career. Honestly speaking, it was not easy to align with his stringent standards and meet his high expectations but I did it in certain projects.

He was always giving me honest feedback just to make me realize where I was lacking and where I fell short of. His approach and manner on how he gave me feedback was extraordinary. He would give me tasks and responsibilities that he saw that I could handle, which I felt in the beginning I could not.

This leader had faith in me and he believed me.

His way may be hard-hitting, frank and pragmatic, which may not sit well with everyone else. But what he aimed to achieve was to hone my skills and develop my talents by assigning me tasks and then giving me constructive criticisms afterwards. In the beginning, he asked me what do I want to become. Then, I told him I want to be a good public speaker.

True enough, he was the first to put me on the spotlight and asked me to co-facilitate with him a training session on the topic of 'How to handle difficult conversations with heads of departments.'

Mr. Charles wanted me to experience first-hand how it is to be out of my comfort zone. Hence, he also paved the way that I will have cross-exposure in corporate office and he gave me the opportunity to visit one of the role model HR team of our company at another location.

Because of that, I met great leaders and teams that I learned very valuable lessons from. Through the process, I was able to build my self-confidence, acquire more knowledge and skills and that is why I am here today.

In relationships like friendships, there are a lot of friends who you think will complement you but in reality, I do think you need friends who will inspire you and not drag you down. If you want to improve your career and stay committed to your passion for learning, you need friends who always will give you honest feedback.

One example here is my close friend Mr. Majeed Al Jabri who is pushing me forward for my career path and learning. He is a very passionate friend and he always let me think how I can be better than I was yesterday, in terms of knowledge.

These types of friendships are the ones we need to improve our quality of learning. Those who will support and guide us through our quest for improvement and success. The one who will complement us and not just offer compliments to us.

In the workplace, I also prefer to have strong employees who are not only kind but those who can push their leader to think and consider different perspectives before making any decision. I always like working with employees who dare to give their honest feedback to their manager or supervisors especially when it comes to doing the right thing.

As you read this book, I have one great person who is helping me finish this book. She is the one who did not accept even single idea to be written in this book without dozens of questions. Always she challenged me on how I write my thoughts and experience by probing me with difficult questions. She tries her best to uncover many details so I can best deliver the wisdom I want to share to my readers. I changed most of the titles because of her questions. She is Ms. Monera Lukman who is talented on how to put the sentences in a proper way. I am proud of my decision because I chose the right person to complement me to achieve my goal of writing this book.

Lesson:

The lesson here is that always choose someone stronger than you. Someone who complements you and not just someone who just offers compliments. Treasure this kind of people who may either be your manager, colleagues, relatives, or friends because the values they share and the value they add up to your life will lead you to greater heights and will remain with you for the rest of your life.

Chapter 11
Ideas but No Action
Is Stagnation

One of the things which will keep you in the same level and will never let you go forward is when you think a thousand times and your actions remains ZERO. Actually, it is one of the most challenging habits many people are facing, either entrepreneurs or employees. It can affect even their social life too. Generally, this matter makes the difference in the success of these people especially in the business and workplace.

I must admit that one of my weaknesses before was this. I was thinking a thousand times without taking even one single action. This overthinking with no actions leads to stagnation. Actually, I realized I was suffering too much because I was busy in my mind only. Later on, I discovered that you must take actions because it is our action that will push us forward, regardless if we pass or fail.

Maybe you are asking now in a critical way, "What if I fail?" To be honest, this is one of the possible consequences that you must be ready to accept. Because the only time that you will have real-life experience is first, you must take action, then be ready for the consequences… it will result in either something positive or something negative. The best thing is that you are already practicing the 70% part of learning. Rather than being stagnant and just be where you are, you must break the status quo. You must rock the boat.

Based on what I have learned, the common ground of the many books I have read which is similar to the success stories of people around me is that they think, plan, and take actions then they will evaluate what they did. After evaluating, they then take better actions to get fruitful results.

Lesson:

You should have the skill to monitor the balance of what you think you should do and the actions you take. Despite what you are thinking about. It is very important to see where you were and where you are today. Be bold to take actions despite what are the potential risks but make sure all that will take you somewhere, you will be proud of yourself.

Formula

Think + Think + Think = Stagnation
Think + Actions + Think = Results

Chapter 12
It Is Time to Decide

One of the challenging moments I have to face is when I have to make a crucial decision but I feel I am in the gray area where I do not know whether to go right or left. I feel a tremendous degree of pressure especially if I do not know what to decide.

Therefore, after several times of struggling, it was at this critical stage that I told myself that I have to face this challenge and learn how to handle it. I am sure there are other people out there who are suffering the same dilemma I have been through up to this date.

I believe, just like me, they are also looking for ways or solution on how to win this battle and be more proactive on how to make their decision whether it involves their personal or professional affairs.

In my career journey, I was struggling a lot when I had to handle difficult cases. Especially the cases when critical decisions were to be made. You cannot imagine I was thinking about them 24/7 and I felt that I was trapped in a prison. My mistake was that I was thinking about the consequences already in a complicated way or extremely exaggerated manner. As time went by, and as I evolved in my professional career, I realized one thing. Decision-making needs to be actively practiced to reach that level where you can make your decisions fast in a critical time.

Actually, it is not 100% blindly but with little study and with clear idea of the consequences wherein you can take ownership of your decision and take the full responsibility of its consequences.

In my own point of view, the real leaders are the ones who can give their team the leverage to practice on making their decisions no matter what its impact is. I worked in more than five companies and I observed that the major difference from team to team is how they feel responsible of their actions, how much space they are given to take decisions, and how much room they are allotted to be involved in each single challenge of the team.

Lesson:

Decision-making is not about the kind of decisions you have to make, whether it is easy or difficult, because there is no guarantee on what the results will be. But it is more about how you will take the consequences after making your decisions, whether it is up or down.

What will set you apart is if you have accepted the challenge of decision-making from the beginning, then later on, as you continuously put it into practice, this decision-making skill, coupled with your experience and gut-feeling, will guide you on how you can arrive at decisions least likely to have negative consequences or liabilities.

Chapter 13
He Said, 'You Are Not Stable'

The one thing in this life which I like is the ability to see the difference in each person's perspectives. I have observed that there are many people who stop doing what they love because someone voiced out about being skeptic towards what he is doing or he had been criticized on what he chose to do in his life.

This is why we need to understand what does it mean by the difference in perspective? How should we deal with it? For me, it is a critical art to practice and master, as it will help you to be yourself and follow your path towards your journey to success.

From my personal experience, I heard many times these words being thrown at me, 'you are not stable' basically because I changed my job more than five times in a span of ten years. I was smiling at them because they did not understand that it was one of the bravest steps I had decided to take to skip many levels and this is why I am here today. I do not want to boast about my position, but I reached the manager position after five years of working because I moved from one job to another.

I know each one of us has his or her own way to achieve what his or her goal. I had already accepted that even before I heard these words because I knew that they do not see what I see and what I feel. I answered to one of them: "There is a big difference in the meanings of 'what is stable' between you and me," and then I smiled.

You have to believe that you cannot make all people agree with you and this is part of life. This is why we need to consider this as something positive that we have to acknowledge and accept that we have different opinions, beliefs, and perspectives on how we plan our life and our future.

Do not allow to be derailed or disheartened when someone questions or doubts your decisions in life. My advice is, as long as you have clearly weighed the pros and cons of your decisions, go ahead with it.

Lesson:

You should have your own way to achieve what you want. Put trust and faith on yourself that you will be able to go ahead. Believe me when I tell you that mimicking others will lead you to fail most of the time.

Chapter 14
Learning Journey or
Fake Journey

I met a lot of various kinds of people throughout my career up to this date. Many times, I was taken aback when I heard someone asserting himself and saying, "I am an expert." When I hear these words, I just shake my head as usual.

After sometime, I noticed that they are not describing themselves but the quantity of years that they have been in the company which they did not add value on it after the first year. Unfortunately, some people, they do not know where they are exactly and the most horrible part is that, they do not know what they need to improve on to be in the next level. For me, I call this as fake journey.

In the fake journey, this is when we do not find ways to be able to reach our goal. We just imagine it every day but we are in no way near it because we do not start doing something about it. Also, the bigger problem lies if we keep trying to mimic someone else. If we will do this, we will be forever in the same room. In this room, we will never try something new or we will not face new challenges that will enable us to change our destination from fake to the learning journey.

I am sure you are wondering as I did when I met someone who blindly says he is an expert but obviously he does not know. So, do you think this person is in the learning journey, or is he on a fake journey?

By the way, in the real learning journey, there is stage where we need to go through checkpoints which I call self-audit. These checkpoints are part of your learning journey when a person assesses where he is, what level did he reach, and what he needs to do be able to achieve his goal. This self-audit will also take these people out of the fake learning journey and drag them back to the right track of the real learning journey.

I am not surprised, because if you look at these people, just assess their environment and see the kind of people who are around them. You will see by the kind of people you go with and the kind of environment you surround yourself with. This will help you determine if you are in the right way of learning journey or not.

I remember my dad when I was in 4th grade, he told me, "Every weekend, I will give you one English sentence and you need to know it by heart. Then I will give the next one after another, for you to have dozens of English sentences."

In those times of my life what I realized was that it is better that you add something of value even if it just a simple act.

"Something is better than nothing." This mantra has been inculcated in my mind because of my father. Looking back at that moment, I can tell you that because of him teaching me one step at a time, I developed the habit of adding more English words to my vocabulary.

Until I reached the level when I have had the capacity to acquire more tools such as books, audio materials, videos, and other means, with my dedication to push myself to learn English more and more consistent in me because I learned the value of it at such a tender age. This is one aspect of my learning journey.

Lesson:

What I learned from my dad is that learning needs to be measured by progress. Therefore, we need to know how much we are doing to be able to go forward and to keep moving on without giving up.

The learning journey is not measured by the number of years you have devoted working for a company but it is measured by the value you added to your skills and knowledge in order to become a better person than you were yesterday.

Chapter 15
Growth Feedback

Long time back, I was annoyed of many things especially, I remember, when my father and mother questioned me what I was doing… like why I never study and why I do bad things.

As I matured, I became aware and acknowledged all of their advices and if I had followed them early on, I might have become much better. Yes, before, I felt angry when someone advised me because I was looking at it as something not good at all.

Unfortunately, at that time, I did not see at what was beyond those advices. Actually, I was thinking before that those advices were just mere words. However, realizing it now, their advice and feedback were something bigger which could have driven me towards growth.

Time and again, we need to distinguish between a growth feedback and a destructive feedback. Here is one story: when I was sitting with a group of people at a dining table. One of them asked another person, "Are you working?"

"Yes, I am working in that place which is very far from my home," he said.

Then, the first person replied, "Oops, if I were you, I will not accept that even if they gave me very high salary."

Imagine what could have happened if that person listened and took seriously this guy's advice and then decided to leave his job?

Feedback are not only the words which we say directly but sometimes within these words, it will discourage people to go forward. I worked in more than five companies and I heard different kinds of destructive feedback that kept people down. These destructive feedbacks came either from managers or workmates.

In contrast, growth feedback is positive because it offers you alternative solutions and not only to say 'not good'. There is a huge difference when you enlighten someone's life and when you keep someone in gray area in his life.

When I joined one of the companies, one of employees came to my office and he said to me, "Are you crazy to work here?" Imagine on your first day at work, I heard this feedback about the company.

If I was the type of person who gets easily affected by this kind of feedback, I would have been taken aback and might not have continue as I did.

This is why we should have strong foundation of positivity and have that firm belief to go forward without easily being affected by such words and destructive feedback.

Chapter 16
MBA Journey

I consider my MBA journey one of my biggest accomplishments that I am proud of, at the same time humbled that I have accomplished after hundreds of challenges and setbacks.

Truth be told, my first challenge was how to pay the exorbitant fees for this MBA school which I chose. To be honest, I do not know how it happened that I was able to settle it. I consider it a miracle.

Here I can say, it is important that you plan your goals and start putting them in writing. You can write it on paper, in your notebook, or in your dream box where you can see them every day. It was by divine intervention or by whatever 'force' that attracted me to it, suddenly I realized, I was already attending my MBA classes.

While it was happening, I was looking at it as very long and arduous journey because several times, I wanted to stop and give up many times. Studying and at the same time working, is never easy at all… especially when I was working long hours and sometimes I used my sleeping time just to study and then go to my work without sleeping overnight.

There were many stories which I cannot put in details here. Many nights and days I felt I was alone and I did not know what should I do as the deadline of projects were very tight. Not to mention that my mood was up and down and sometimes I got to the point that I felt very confused and anxious.

Imagine, you have to conquer the feeling of not being in the mood to study but you have to fight that because you have to submit an assignment. I must say that I achieved this journey not only because of my efforts but because I surrounded myself with great people who I owed a lot for giving me their valuable time, support, and efforts.

They are the very people who liked to see me go up the stage of graduation ceremony. It is noteworthy to mention here that in the last year of my MBA journey, I had a manager who was not supportive at all. That was the reason why I never informed him that I was studying on the side. Because of this challenge, I doubled or even tripled my efforts to work harder to not show him that my productivity at work is not going down.

It was not easy at all to do that but I forced myself to make it happen without his support. And today I can say thank you to him as his difficult personality was part of my lessons. I did not only learn theoretically and academically from this MBA experience but I also learned from real-life battlefield scenarios.

You have to be passionate in what you are doing to be able to survive. It is good that it came natural to me that I loved my job and the same time I loved studying so I was able to beat the challenges along the way. What a great and awesome feeling it was to be on the stage during my graduation ceremony where I felt exceptionally proud and happy of myself.

Looking back, I am thinking that it was just like a dream because the time flew very fast. I learned a lot in this journey as it was not only about theories and concepts of MBA but about also about building my character.

I learned about gratitude, commitment, humility, passion, patience, and resilience. These are great values that are very important for us to possess and to practice if we want to reach our goals in life.

The lesson is that having a plan is the key to achieving our goals. During the execution of your plan, there will be a big door that will open for you wherein you will gain many things and not only the one thing you are aiming for.

Moreover, you cannot achieve this goal alone but you need to be humble enough to say I do not know and please guide me, please lend me a helping hand. By this way, you will be able see what you cannot see.

Inspired of the fact that you are smart or strong, you still need people to give you support otherwise you will not reach the place where you are heading to.

Finally, time is wealth if you know how to value and use it. Time, if you know how to manage it, will enable you to reach the destination that you are aiming for. Just plan and love what you have planned for you to enjoy the journey.

Chapter 17
The Horrible Boss: Get the Best from Them

I am wondering, is it fair to label someone as a horrible boss or a bad manager? Because when we say bad, it is a general word which will not be fair to describe a manager or more or less, even generalize most of our managers as such.

I have worked in more than five companies and I can say that from each one of my managers, I learned something beneficial for me no matter their way was good or bad.

However, I do understand that just like you, sometimes I do feel depressed, stressed, sad and down because of their way.

Actually, I realize that it is because, first, sometimes we do not know how to deal with these people. This is why we need to go deep and look beyond their words and actions to understand them. There you might see something good.

Second, our expectations on them may be too high as we expect them to be perfect and to know it all.

You know why I put this topic in my book? It is because this topic, our manager, is a big part of our working life. In fact, their impact to us also transcends beyond that – they even affect our personal lives.

I met a lot of people who are not feeling well at home, on the road or at work because of the challenging relationship they have with their managers. Therefore, we need to fix it ASAP.

I know someone who became sick because of this matter and he kept mentioning his manager in every single conversation when I'd meet him.

To be honest, here I can say you should find a way to either fight or flight. Fight in a way that you engage in a difficult conversation with your manager. Open up what is bothering you and express your sentiments in a good way. Or if you think that it will not be productive to do so, just let it be and leave it. Flight. Move on.

Actually, to be honest, I was one of those who struggled with having horrible bosses. But after a long time of experience, I built my own way on how to deal with them. For me, the most or should I say the best experience I got from it, it gave me many skills on how to make the whole experience interesting despite the difficult situations.

Strong and tough manager is not bad, because in reality, it is in this way that we will learn how to push ourselves to our limit, we will be challenged to think out of the box, and to stand for what we believe is right.

Actually, sometimes, there are repercussions when we work with overly kind manager because we tend to be complacent and to stay in our comfort zone.

Thus it is better for us to accept what is the leadership style of our manager whether we see it as good or bad, and we just get the best out of it. As it is, your working relationship is just a transit, as people will come and go. Better make the most of it and take the best out of it.

One of my best friends advised me and he imparted to me this good advice. He said, "Do not leave your company because of your manager but because of something different like your desire to face new challenges or a higher offer."

Lesson:

Our work-life is a big chunk of our life story which gives meaning to our life and this is how it is for most people.

You need to see the value and the lessons you can take from your relationship with your manager which can improve your work life and personal life.

Work life is a valuable experience and always remember that tomorrow you might become a manager too. Do not repeat the experiences that gave a negative impact on you with the subordinates that will be under you. Do not repeat the past mistakes as it happens with some people. Put in mind that the manager position is not permanent, it is merely temporary. Therefore, think on how to add value to others, either by easy way or difficult way.

Chapter 18
Plan, So Less Pain

This topic keeps nagging my mind every day; therefore, it is crucial for every single project in my life to have a PLAN. When I remember any project that I could not accomplish, I observe that having no plan was the major reason that led that project to fail.

There are many questions that we should ask ourselves and our team before we start any project and most of them are related to planning. Every single step should be planned and with corresponding timeline otherwise even the commitment level will go down after some time.

Thus, all projects need to have a plan in order to achieve them. And take note, it's not necessary to achieve it successfully. I mean that sometimes the project will not be achieved or go as planned but something great that will come out of it anyhow. You will gain valuable lessons, experience, and knowledge.

More than five years ago, I dreamed of having a business of my own. Then I started my business without a good plan and feasibility study. Yes, in the beginning, the business was going well and it was profitable.

Suddenly, I got sick and I could not continue because there was no continuity plan. Thus, my business did not prosper and I lost my customers.

From this tough experience, what I put in my mind was, never will I think negatively about this experience. Somehow, I learned something and I achieved understanding. It was never too late to start over again.

In my career path, I have had many projects which I could not finish properly. This is why I was suffering because I was working like fireman at the nick of time. I remember that many times I was working overnight and I was annoyed. Sometimes we blame others like our managers or companies where we work and even our family because our expectations are not reached.

However, the real reason is that we do not plan our projects very well or the more dangerous part, the projects are executed without any plan at all.

I do not mean here only big projects but small daily projects. Here we should be conscious about practicing planning to make sure those small projects are successful and will lead us to become a good planner if later on, we have big projects.

In addition, if you have a team and you do not put proper plan for them, you will actually drag them to be lost and when we hear managers say that their team are not performing well, we need to ask and double-check if there is daily plan, monthly, and yearly plan. Then we can conclude and we can say if their manager was right or not.

Here is a good story where I planned to close two loans in four years. This was one of the projects I am proud to tell you about and this month is the last installment. If you ask me,

"Was it easy?" My answer is "NO" but what a feeling when you plan for something which you planned since couple of years and you have now done successfully. Especially this type of plan which improved your quality of life. Many people think to plan only for business but it is not right, you also have to plan for your personal life too.

The good news for me is that in 2020 I put my plan for ten years where I see myself there in this journey. This plan helps me to be careful and wise in my every single step and hopefully will help me to write a book about it in future.

Lesson:

It is better to have a bad plan than to have no plan at all. When you plan your projects, that means you enlighten your dark ways and the people around you. Planning is the best tool to get the right experience with even those projects that are not successful.

I can summarize here in below formula:

Great Plan = great experience.

No Plan = painful regret if you fail.

Chapter 19
30s Age

Why do I want to talk about age? Particularly the age I am in. Though we do not want to set limit to the possibilities that we can achieve; however, our age is such a limiting force that realistically we have to deal with it. Because whether we like it or not, our life is time-bound. Our life will end, our body will age, our physical strength will deteriorate, our hair will turn gray, our eyes will blur… these are the realities of life.

There is something in our age that must serve as our timeline for ourselves. The sooner we realize that the better. Because we do not want to wake up one day only to realize we are almost on the finishing line, and ask ourselves where are all those good years have gone?

I consider that the 30s age is a great opportunity to plan and put our plan into action if we did not start planning our goals during our 20s. When I was in my 20s, my mindset was that I was always in a hurry to finish and to reach what I wanted, but I can say it was not well-supported with skills, knowledge, and experience. So it did not sustain me well and I did not succeed. I must say, the end result was not of good quality.

Actually for me, the 30s age is a good beginning of plan and start of achieving your goals. But I can hear others telling me now that in this age, you are still young, no need to think of serious stuff yet, it is early to plan for retirement and so on.

But I believe, the 30s age is the time to put plan for retirement because it is more about stability. I'm now 35 years old and I can say that 30s age is more about achieving and earning more. Earning not only in terms of money but knowledge. It is more about equipping yourself with the right tools and seeking the help of the right people to help achieve the results that you want.

It is my execution stage, wherein I need to execute what I want. Such as I want to have a business, I want to have a savings plan and I also find it is the age for habit correction.

The habit that I wanted to change is 'to stop doing things randomly and to really practice time management on how I conduct my day'.

I remembered when I was in my 20s, my way of thinking and reaction for every single case was out-of-hand or exaggerated. But in my 30s, I think more before I act and react. I feel that I become more responsible and accountable unlike when I was in 20s. Your 30s is the time for self-reflection—to put yourself to the right track. They say, age is just a number. Yes, it is just a number. You should not feel your age. But not to do something for your future thinking you will be forever young is a mindset doomed for failure. You have to own your 30s age and accept that but you should use this time wisely while balancing on the limitless mindset.

I see and hear people who surpassed 30s age, they wish to go back to beginning of 30s to amend many things. Today I am dreaded by thoughts that passing your 30s without accomplishing anything is dreadful. I can see myself there in post-thirties age and feel extremely happy thinking how if I really reach there where I can have great feelings of financial security, emotional stability, and professional success.

85

Lesson:

Your 30s age is a stage to correct the things you have done incorrectly in the past and to open your world to big opportunities to achieve your goals. This is the age that you have to think on how to live your life how you want it.

Regardless of others' opinions and dogmas. It is really the right age to focus on planning and organizing your life, give priorities to plan for your savings and retirement. Perceive this age as the right time to rewrite your story in a great and right way.

Chapter 20
Covid-19 Pandemic
A Change Revolution

Coronavirus or better known as Covid-19, the pandemic that brought a tremendous impact and changed on how we live our lives, wreaked havoc across the world. We had never imagined that year 2020 will be life-changing and beginning and ending like that. The year 2020 was such an unforgettable year as it brought and caused so many changes, uncertainties and instability. Our lives were forever changed because of this pandemic. For me, I call it a change revolution.

Just like anyone else, when this Coronavirus started spreading here and there, it came as a shock to me and to the people around me. At first, the virus began in one marketplace in one country, then suddenly it spread so fast that without any prior warning, it reached our very own country… and then it burst into a global phenomenon… that's why it was called a pandemic.

If I recollect my memory of those days when we were hearing about this virus, I was giving advice and precaution to my colleagues to be careful on how to avoid contracting it. Some of them did not take me seriously and some were in fact laughing at me. Not until we all realized the gravity of this pandemic then that was the time when we took it more seriously after hearing that the virus is highly contagious and many countries are advising their citizens to wear face masks, use face shields, not to go out of their houses, telling them that the food will be delivered at their doorstep. Then country-lockdown came into in our vocabulary.

Here the story started when my ears started waiting for bad news about how many cases and number of deaths in a daily basis here in Oman and other countries. In addition, rumors came from here and there, and true enough, this became worse in this scenario. When you are hearing stories about people who suffered difficulty of breathing, then suddenly they were in ICU, then they die. The worse thing was when they couldn't even be visited by their loved ones.

Imagine most people were in a state of panic in the workplace, at home and in the road. I know some people did test more than three times because they became more anxious and scared. I was hearing each mourning from the people around me, "This time, I am sure I have COVID-19."

On a personal note, I experienced the same. I felt I had the symptoms of COVID, I had terrible headache, body pain and cough. The funny thing is when I did my swab test the first time. I was sure and I had no tinge of doubt that I have it but the result came out negative. And then again the second time, I could not sleep the night before but the result was the same, it was negative. I experienced the same feeling of anxiety and fear that I felt I was positive but it turned out I was negative.

Then you hear stories of family, friends and former colleagues about their companies cutting down on salaries and some people forcibly being terminated because the company couldn't support that number of workforce.

Suddenly, you are just worried about being infected and your loved ones or your colleagues being covid-positive. More than that, your worries extended beyond… you do not feel secure anymore with the job that you have.

All that happened with me and the people around me; I said to myself 'stop', and I asked myself some questions: *Is this feeling because of the pandemic? What should I do? If I panic, what will happen?*

Then I decided to write down all my goals and I kept looking at them and I wrote things which I really wanted. I started to focus more about these opportunities which reduced the potential threats like losing my job or whatever I was worried about. All such questions dragged me to the right track where I could see the clear future with what I wanted.

One of the things I learned in this pandemic is that nothing is permanent and we need to have alternatives to keep moving especially with the ways to reach our goals. You need to have options. This is why I found another way to reach my goals. This pandemic taught me that the crisis is testing your passion about what you called your goals.

We need to put in our mind that each crisis here is to exercise our brain and to keep our heart resilient to make us ready for the journey, to make us stronger not weaker. It is all about mindset.

I have real example without mentioning their names, I have someone very close to me and in the middle of 2020, the company where this person works decided to stop giving the employees their salary. I expected this person will go back to his country but he refused to go back. He told me one day, "I am learning to enjoy the basic things."

My reaction was just, I said, "You are really strong because I cannot imagine that for myself."

In this pandemic, there are many champions we need to learn from because they are giving us strong lessons which will push us to go forward patiently. All the more what we need in this pandemic is to be positive and to have hope.

It is easy to succumb to negativity and depression but you need to look at the people around you. Take a look at how people handle the crisis well and emulate them. We need to be remaining hopeful. Thus in the end, there are some people who will pass this pandemic successfully and unfortunately it will not end will for those who are thinking the opposite.

By the way, I have initiated my own program to keep me going in the right track during this pandemic. Here we can go as we create something new and it is suitable for us to bring back the same passion we had before this pandemic.

Lesson:

Remember that crisis is just temporary no matter how long it takes. First, we need to find ways that are suitable for us to minimize the potential risks. Second, look at the crisis as a potential growth area and not something that will destroy us. Third, take note, there are many ways to dive on it.

I learned that when you feel there is no option, that means you are only thinking that there is only one way to make it happen. Just dare to think of other options and go for what is best.

Finally, crisis is a stopover for self-reflection, where we might need to change our course, our path, to reach our destination. This pandemic is a crisis that will need a change, a revolution. Accept the crisis, adapt to the 'new normal' and make the changes.

Crises are opportunities more than they are threats.

During crises, we need to rely on new methods than old methods.